THE WORLD OF NASCAR

UNDER THE HELMET:
Inside the Mind of a Driver

TRADITION BOOKS®
A New Tradition in Children's Publishing™
MAPLE PLAIN, MINNESOTA

BY CURT CAVIN

Published by **Tradition Books**® and distributed to the
school and library market by **The Child's World**®
P.O. Box 326
Chanhassen, MN 55317-0326
800/599-READ
http://www.childsworld.com

Photo Credits
Cover: AP/Wide World
AP/Wide World: 6, 9, 17, 20, 25
Sports Gallery: 5, 11, 13, 16, 22, 23 (Al Messerschmidt), 7, 8, 10, 14, 19, 26, 27 (Brian Spurlock)

An Editorial Directions book
Editorial Directions, Inc.: E. Russell Primm, Editorial Director; Katie Marsico and Elizabeth K.
Martin, Assistant Editors; Olivia Nellums, Editorial Assistant; Susan Hindman, Copy Editor;
Susan Ashley, Proofreader; Kevin Cunningham, Fact Checker; Tim Griffin/IndexServ, Indexer;
James Buckley Jr., Photo Researcher and Selector

The Design Lab: Kathy Petelinsek, Art Director and Designer; Kari Thornborough,
Page Production

Library of Congress Cataloging-in-Publication Data
Cavin, Curt.
  Under the helmet : inside the mind of a driver / by Curt Cavin.
    p. cm. — (The world of NASCAR)
Summary: Looks at the thoughts and decisions of thirty-year-old Matt Kenseth, a racecar
driver on the NASCAR Winston Cup circuit, during a race near Phoenix, Arizona. Includes
bibliographical references (p.) and index.
  ISBN 1-59187-036-4
  1. Automobile racing drivers—Juvenile literature. 2. NASCAR (Association)—Juvenile litera-
ture. [1. Kenseth, Matt. 2. Automobile racing drivers. 3. Automobile racing.] I. Title. II. Series.
GV1029.13
.C38 2003 796.72'092—dc21   2003008444

Note: Beginning with the 2004 season, the NASCAR
Winston Cup Series will be called the NASCAR Nextel
Cup Series.

UNDER THE HELMET

Table of Contents

4   **Introduction:** The Show Goes On

6   **Chapter One:** The Start

11   **Chapter Two:** Racing the Track

17   **Chapter Three:** The Decisions

23   **Chapter Four:** The Finish

29   Matt Kenseth's "Office"

30   Glossary

31   For More Information about NASCAR Racing

32   Index

The Show Goes On

T he drivers on the **NASCAR Winston Cup** circuit have been racing since February, when the season opened with the Daytona 500. During the first week of November, they gather at a track 10 miles (16 kilometers) west of Phoenix, Arizona. The Checker Auto Parts 500 is the 35th race in a difficult 36-race schedule. The competitors are tired.

Racing almost every weekend for 10 months is a grind unlike no other in sports. Drivers and their crews get a day off on Mother's Day in May and another in late June. This is the 19th different state in the fourth different time zone. People are tired from all the miles put on in airplanes and on the track. They want to go home and rest. They want to hunt, fish, play golf, watch television, and enjoy life with their children, wives, and dogs. But today, despite being weary, they must race. The show must go on.

Matt Kenseth, a 30-year-old driver from Cambridge, Wisconsin, isn't sure how he feels. On one hand, he is eager to try for his series-leading fifth victory. On the other hand, he is mentally tired and is fighting the sniffles from allergies caused by the desert air. His nose and his body say "stop," but his head says "go." Like the other drivers, he goes anyway. Today, it's full speed ahead, for better or worse. "This is as good as I'm going to feel," he says. "Let's go."

Matt Kenseth is one of the hottest young drivers in NASCAR's Winston Cup Series.

CHAPTER ONE

The Start

Coming into the Phoenix race, Matt Kenseth had won only one **pole** in his 112 Winston Cup races. That pole came at Dover Downs in Delaware in June 2002. The number-one starting position did not guarantee him a good finish, however. He ended up 40th in that race.

Actually, some of Kenseth's worst qualifying positions have come in the races he has won. He started 21st when he won his first race at Charlotte, North Carolina, in May 2000. In fact, he started no better than 20th in his next five victories. "It's not how you start," Kenseth says on the morning of the race, "it's how you finish."

Matt squirts soda on his crew as they celebrate his victory at Charlotte in 2000.

The problem with starting so far back in a Winston Cup race is the congestion that comes from 43 cars squeezed together. The problem is worse on a narrow track such as the 1-mile (1.6-km) oval at Phoenix. Kenseth will begin from the outside of the 14th row in 28th place. NASCAR lines up its cars in rows of two, based on their speed in qualifying. Kenseth is alongside 2000 NASCAR champion Dale Jarrett and directly behind Ward Burton, winner of the 2002 Daytona 500.

When the **green flag** drops for the 312-lap race, Kenseth is as patient as he can be. He doesn't try to advance too quickly too soon. Instead, he follows Burton as soon as he can, moving ahead of Jarrett on the third lap. Kenseth is on his way to the front!

The track in Phoenix is set beneath dusty desert hills studded with cacti and scrub brush.

Positions are difficult to come by at first, as every driver has the same goal: get to the lead. Kenseth grabs 26th place from Rusty Wallace on the eighth lap and snares two more spots over the next 12 laps. He is 23rd by lap 22 and 22nd by lap 25.

Benny Parsons, who won NASCAR's top division in 1973, knows the frustration that Kenseth and others in the pack are dealing with. "In heavy traffic, these are the most nerve-wracking laps there are," he says. "You have to be patient."

Matt found himself in the middle of the pack early in the race at Phoenix, trailing No. 88, Dale Jarrett.

Kenseth and his crew are trying to be just that. The

yellow caution flag comes out when rookie driver Jamie

McMurray spins out. Kenseth brings his No. 17 yellow-and-

black car down **pit road** for service. But as other teams put

on four new tires, Kenseth's team bolts on just two. This short-

cut allows them to send the car back out sooner, and he gains

11 positions. Now, Kenseth is in tenth place on a crowded track.

This means he is in front of many of the possible problems that

could crop up. It's comforting, although he knows that having

two older tires might cost him speed later in the race. For now,

it's a risk worth taking. "[Being near the front] gives you a better

chance to avoid trouble and race the leaders better," he says.

**The yellow caution flag is waved as an accident occurs
in a NASCAR race. The caution flag slows the race
down until the track is cleared.**

THE PIT CREW

A driver usually wonders what kind of service he will get from his pit crew. But Matt Kenseth doesn't; he knows he has the fastest-working crew in the sport.

Kenseth's crew is nicknamed the Killer Bees for the way it swarms the No. 17 car on stops. It has won the past two World Pit Crew Championships. In 2002, it broke its own record with a stop of 16.832 seconds. In that brief time, the crew changed four tires, fueled the car, and got Kenseth back on the track.

A pit crew includes two tire changers (one each for the front and the rear of the car) and two tire carriers. Another person jacks the car off the ground. In the back are a fuel man and a catch-can man, who catches the leftover fuel and holds a second can of gas.

Each crew member also works on the car at the team's shop during the week. Crew chief Robbie Reiser says working on pit road is something anyone could learn to do. "I remember when we all started, we were all new at this," he says. "We stayed together and just kept on practicing."

Kenseth's crew practices twice a day, three times a week. As they've shown, practice makes perfect.

Count the seven "over the wall" members (in helmets) of Matt Kenseth's pit crew. Matt's crew is one of the best in NASCAR.

CHAPTER TWO

Racing the Track

Passing other cars is not the main concern for Matt
Kenseth in the first half of the Phoenix race. His priori-
ty: figuring out the conditions of the racetrack and
what his car needs to go as fast as possible.

In this case, it seems the No. 17 car likes it when the left-
side tires are more worn than the right-side tires. That way,

The tires on the left side of Matt's car wear down
more than the right. That helps Matt grip the road
better in turns.

the car has more grip with the asphalt, particularly coming off the second and fourth corners. Excelling at these spots is critical to maximizing speed on the fast **straightaways** at Phoenix.

"You want to get into turn one good so you can carry a lot of momentum off the second turn," says Kenseth. He is referring to an odd hitch in the Phoenix **backstretch.** "If you come off turn two [too slowly], the car will bog down on the back straightaway. I want to get [the engine] wide open early in the corner so that doesn't happen."

On this day, Kenseth makes several passes entering the third turn because he has more speed than most of his rivals. In other words, how he has driven through the first turn has helped him get off the second turn better. This lets him pass other cars entering the third turn. The idea of gaining speed out of turns is true on most racetracks.

The Phoenix track is located in the desert west of the city. Dust and high air temperature combine to make the asphalt surface particularly slippery. The tires do not make good enough contact with the road, and drivers wrestle the steering

wheel to keep from crashing. The crews try to fix the problem

by putting more air pressure in the tires and adjusting the

This photo shows the main straightaway at the Phoenix track. The large white structure in the stands contains the press box and announcers' booth.

By lap 79, Matt is moving up and is now among the leaders of the race.

weight of the cars. But sometimes they go too far, as many have on this day. Brakes and tire rubber have been lost, and the handling characteristics of the cars have changed for the worse.

"The [car] gets tight and won't turn in the middle of the corner," says John Andretti. The veteran driver qualified second but was losing positions by the handful in the race. "It's typical of Phoenix. That's what separates the good cars from the great cars."

Kenseth has one of the great cars in this race. After moving up to tenth place with the two-tire pit stop, he is slowly but surely passing other cars in front of him. After telling the crew that he "likes the way it's going," Kenseth overtakes Elliott Sadler for seventh on lap 52. On lap 79, he nabs the sixth spot from rookie Ryan Newman.

Kenseth is getting more in tune with the racetrack as time goes by. The better he can "race the track," as drivers say, the better he can race against other drivers.

HELMET RADIOS

Drivers and crew members wear two-way radios during practices and races. A driver tells the crew chief how the car is performing; the crew chief tells the driver what he can (or can't) do to improve the situation. The radios are also used to alert the driver to problems on the track, such as accidents or debris out of his view. Most of this kind of information comes from **spotters** in seats high above the track.

Fans at home can sometimes listen in. Television producers can broadcast some of the radio chatter to the TV audience.

Technically, the radios are simple systems. The driver listens through an earpiece and talks through a microphone inside his helmet. He presses a button on the steering wheel when he wants to talk. When a driver is quiet on the radio, that usually means he is busy. It might also mean he's very happy with the way the car is working.

The wire leading into Mark Martin's ear is his connection to his crew. The microphone he uses is built into his helmet.

C H A P T E R   T H R E E

The Decisions

Pit stops in racing appear pretty simple. The driver heads down pit road, gets tires and fuel, and returns to the track. But, of course, it is not that easy. And choosing when to make a stop is even more difficult.

Crew chiefs and drivers begin plotting pit strategy before the race weekend starts. In Kenseth's case, he and crew chief Robbie Reiser learned from a mistake that cost them a victory. At Talladega in April, they had made a mistake in their fuel use. Now they are

Matt's crew chief Robbie Reiser (left) makes the decisions about the pit crew during a race.

17

focused on having just enough fuel to make it to the finish line with as few stops as possible. In this case, if they can reach lap 123 before making their second stop, they can go the rest of the way with just one more stop for fuel. If it works out that there are no more caution flags, they could win because everyone else will have to make two more stops for fuel.

But as so often happens, the plan backfires. As Kenseth crosses the start/finish line past the pit entrance on lap 122, his Ford runs out of gas. He has to **coast** around the track with the engine off. It is a long, quiet ride for Kenseth, who tells Reiser on the radio that the chance to win is gone. "We ran three laps longer than we should have," Kenseth says. "We went one lap too (far)."

Reiser isn't willing to give up just yet. "Keep your head," he tells Kenseth on the radio. "If we can get some cautions and have some things go our way, we can (recover)."

Kenseth keeps the faith and keeps battling. After filling up, he roars back to the track. After a caution comes a few laps

After coasting in to fill up with gas, Matt roared back into the race, chasing the leaders.

A later crash by NASCAR rookie Christian Fittipaldi (GP car) gives Matt the chance to make a key pit stop.

later and all the leaders pit again, he is in 11th place. More than half the race remains, and he knows he has a good car. He passes Jeff Burton for the ninth position on lap 156. He moves around Dale Earnhardt Jr., whose car is slipping all over the track, on lap 167.

Kenseth gets the third spot behind leaders Kurt Busch and Jeff Gordon just before the final round of pit stops. When Christian Fittipaldi crashes, everyone comes down pit road for the final service of the race. Almost everyone takes four tires. Reiser, knowing how good the car was earlier on two tires, takes a chance and tries it again. It's a crucial decision. Choosing the wrong tire switch now could cost Kenseth the race.

Reiser's team makes the two-tire switch, and his driver is rewarded instantly. Zooming off pit road, Matt Kenseth has the lead with 52 laps to go. "I thought it was a good idea," Kenseth says. Now, can he hold the lead with others behind him having fresher tires?

DRIVER FATIGUE

About halfway into a race, drivers begin to feel tired. Their arms are sore from wrestling the heavy car around the tight track. Their concentration needs a break from focusing on what seems to be never-ending traffic. On a warm day, they are hot, thirsty, and ready for a breather. Pit stops aren't really a break because they are so short (16 to 18 seconds) and the driver is still busy controlling the car.

Although drivers carry water bottles near them in the cars, they don't drink until the caution flag comes out. Even then, there is not a lot of spare time. Drivers spend most of the slow-down time talking with their crew chief. They discuss changes to make to the car during the pit stop. There certainly is not time to eat.

Occasionally, on a really hot day, drivers need to get out of the car to keep from overheating and fainting. In such cases, teams find other drivers in the garage to take their place. On a pit stop, the regular driver is helped from the car and the replacement driver jumps in. It takes several seconds to make the exchange, including the time-consuming procedure of fastening the seat belts. However, a relief driver is better than a dangerously hot driver.

A driver's cockpit is a tight fit. He is held tightly in place by a five-point seating harness. The seat is inside a heavy metal roll cage.

CHAPTER FOUR

The Finish

Matt Kenseth likes the two-tire decision Robbie Reiser made on the final pit stop. The move gave Kenseth the lead. At Phoenix, where passing is difficult because of the lack of banking in the corners, being in front is absolutely the place to be.

"At Phoenix, there is a big advantage to being able to use the whole racetrack (without cars in front of you)," Kenseth says. "If you run side-by-side, it really bogs you down coming off turn two. You can lose quite a bit of time on the lap times."

Here's a good look at Matt's Ford Taurus. How many sponsors' stickers can you count on his car? Each one means money in the bank for Matt's team.

Kenseth makes his getaway from Rusty Wallace in second place, who likewise has taken only two tires. Wallace gets stuck racing side-by-side with a **lapped** car. That's just what Kenseth predicted would happen. Wallace's troubles have let Kenseth build a 3-second lead. Wallace wiggles closer, but Kenseth's quick restart is too much to overcome. Wallace is gaining only a tenth of a second on every other lap, not enough to close the gap.

"I didn't expect our car would take off as fast as it did," Kenseth says. "We were worried about the left-side [tires] giving up, but as long as [the race] stayed green, I felt pretty good about winning."

Over the final 10 laps, Kenseth and Wallace run laps at virtually the same speed (123 miles [197 km] per hour). Everything is working out for Kenseth.

His crew members had left their North Carolina homes at 4 A.M. to fly to Phoenix for the afternoon race. They're tired, but they know the long ride home will be easy if they go

Matt's car takes the checkered flag in Phoenix! The
Tide car in the foreground is a lap behind Matt.

This makes all the hard work worthwhile. Matt holds up his winner's trophy after battling to the checkered flag in Phoenix.

home winners. Kenseth fans who have traveled from Wisconsin have reason to smile while wearing foam cheese hats bearing his No. 17. Even Kenseth is starting to feel better. He hasn't noticed his runny nose since he climbed into the car some three hours ago.

Finally, the checkered flag drops as he flashes across the finish line. He wins the race by 1.344 seconds, his fifth victory of the season. No one in Winston Cup has won more this year. Everyone associated with his team smiles and celebrates. He waves his hand out the window as he takes a victory lap. His crew jumps and dances in the pits. It's on to **Victory Lane!**

"This is what we've worked for all week," Kenseth says. "We have a great race team, and I feel so fortunate to have it. I certainly can't do this by myself. It's a team effort!"

It was a team effort that turned into victory after a long day at the track. And you've just had a seat next to the winning driver.

THE FRUITS OF VICTORY

Matt Kenseth kept the giant-size check he received for winning the race, but only as a souvenir. He can't cash it.

The actual check, worth $211,895, will be normal-sized. Kenseth's bosses at Roush Racing will cash it at the bank near their shop in Concord, North Carolina. Matt will get a part of the prize money, with the rest going to the team owners and crew members.

The giant trophy Kenseth received in Victory Lane probably won't stay at his house, either. Typically, three trophies are handed out for the team, driver, and sponsor. The team usually keeps the largest one; the others get a smaller copy.

Kenseth doesn't argue with either long-standing racing practice. The money is still good, the trophy will look great in his den, and the record books will note his accomplishment.

"A win is a win," he says.

Celebration time! Matt and his hard-working crew share in the fun in Victory Lane. Why five fingers? This was Matt's fifth win of the 2002 Winston Cup season.

MATT KENSETH'S "OFFICE"

When a NASCAR driver goes to work, he doesn't sit at a desk in front of an office. He sits inside a welded steel roll cage. His "desk" chair is reinforced aluminum with just a bit of padding. Safety straps keep him tucked and tight in the seat.

Instead of a computer, he watches the dashboard, which includes gauges. (A good trivia note is that your family car's gauges are more high-tech than Matt's. NASCAR rules say all gauges have to use needles, not digital readouts). Here's a look at what's inside Matt's rolling office:

- No speedometer in NASCAR vehicles. Instead drivers watch a "tachome-ter" [tak-OM-itter]. This measures the revolutions per minute (rpms) of the engine.

- No gas gauge. Matt watches a gauge that measures the fuel pressure. If it drops, it's time to call the pit crew on the radio for help!

- No place to put a key! NASCAR vehicles start by flicking switches near the driver.

- Matt also can check the engine temperature and check the car's electrical system.

   (Here's a real "insider's" note: When the needles on all these gauges are straight up and down, they're reading normal. That makes it easy for Matt to glance down quickly and see how things are going. If he had to take time to read numbers, he'd end up somewhere he didn't want to be!)

- Behind him is the oil radiator (which is usually with the engine in "street" cars). This helps make the temperatures in Matt's office as high at 140 degrees F (60 degrees C).

- Above him and in front is a rear-view mirror. This is not your everyday mirror, though. It has three parts that let Matt see cars behind him, to his left, and to his right.

GLOSSARY

backstretch—the long, straight portion of a racetrack opposite the side with the start/finish line

coast—driving a car without the engine on

green flag—signal flag waved to start a race or restart after a caution flag

lapped—when a car has gone ahead of another car by a full lap and then passes it again

NASCAR Winston Cup—the highest level of racing in NASCAR, which stands for the National Association for Stock Car Automobile Racing, created by Bill France Sr. in 1947

pit road—the area of the track where cars go during a race for service

pole—the number-one starting position in a race, usually located on the inside of the first row of cars

spotters—crew members who sit in seats high above the track and radio information to the pit crew

straightaways—in oval racetracks, these are the sides of the track without any curves or turns

Victory Lane—a roped-off or fenced-in area located in the infield of a racetrack where the entire race team and family members celebrate a victory

yellow caution flag—a signal waved to drivers to alert them to danger on the track; all drivers must immediately slow down to the same speed and may not pass until the race is restarted

FOR MORE INFORMATION ABOUT NASCAR RACING

Books

Cavin, Curt. *Race Day: The Fastest Show on Earth.* Excelsior, Minn.: Tradition Books, 2002.

Fleischman, Bill, and Al Pearce. *The Unauthorized NASCAR Fans Guide.* Detroit: Visible Ink Press, 2002.

Huler, Scott. *A Little Bit Sideways.* Osceola, Wis.: MBI Publishing, 1999.

Woods, Bob. *Dirt Track Daredevils: The History of NASCAR.* Excelsior, Minn.: Tradition Books, 2002.

Web Sites

Matt Kenseth's Official Site
http://www.mattkenseth.com
For an in-depth look at everything that has to do with NASCAR driver Matt Kenseth

The Official Web Site of NASCAR
http://www.nascar.com
For an in-depth look at each track on the NASCAR Winston Cup circuit as well as statistical and biographical information on all of the drivers

Phoenix International Raceway
http://www.phoenixinternationalraceway.com
For a complete look at everything that takes place at the Phoenix-area race-track, including schedules, race times, and the latest news

INDEX

Andretti, John, 15

backstretch, 12
Burton, Jeff, 21
Burton, Ward, 7
Busch, Kurt, 21

Checker Auto Parts 500, 4
checkered flag, 27
crew chief, 16, 17, 22s

Dover Downs, 6
driver fatigue, 22

Earnhardt, Dale, Jr., 21

Fittipaldi, Christian, 21
fuel, 10, 17–18
fuel man, 10

Gordon, Jeff, 21
green flag, 7

helmet radios, 16

jack operator, 10
Jarrett, Dale, 7

Kenseth, Matt, 5
cornering, 12
finish, 27
pit stops, 9, 17–18, 21, 23
pole positions, 6, 7
winnings, 28
Killer Bees pit crew, 10

McMurray, Jamie, 9

Newman, Ryan, 15

Parsons, Benny, 8
passing, 12
pit crew, 10, 13, 24, 27
pit stops, 9, 17, 21, 22
pole position, 6

Reiser, Robbie, 10, 17, 18, 21, 23
relief drivers, 22
Roush Racing, 28

Sadler, Elliott, 15
side-by-side racing, 23, 24
spotters, 16
straightaways, 12

team, 9, 10, 21, 27, 28
tire carriers, 10
tire changers, 10
tires, 9, 11–12, 12–13, 15, 21, 24
track conditions, 11, 12–13, 15
trophies, 28

Victory Lane, 27, 28

Wallace, Rusty, 8, 24
Winston Cup Series, 4, 27
World Pit Crew Championships, 10

yellow caution flag, 9, 18, 22

ABOUT THE AUTHOR

Curt Cavin has been a sportswriter for the *Indianapolis Star* since 1987 and has written for *AutoWeek* magazine since 1997. He also does television commentary on racing for WTHR-13 in Indianapolis. His primary assignment is the Indy Racing League, but he also covers NASCAR's Winston Cup division. He also wrote *Terrific Tracks: The Best Places to Race* and *Race Day: The Fastest Show on Earth.* He lives in Indiana with his wife, Becky, and two children, Katie and Quinn.